CATHEDRAL/GROVE

Cathedral/Grove

Poems and drawings by

SUSAN GLICKMAN

THE POETRY IMPRINT AT VÉHICULE PRESS

Published with the generous assistance of the Canada Council for the Arts and the Canada Book Fund of the Department of Canadian Heritage.

 Canada Council Conseil des art
for the Arts du Canada

SIGNAL EDITIONS EDITOR: CARMINE STARNINO

Cover design by David Drummond
Photo of the author by Toan Klein
Set in Minion and Filosofia by Simon Garamond
Printed by Marquis Book Printing Inc.

Dépôt légal, Library and Archives Canada and the Bibliothèque national du Québec, third trimester 2023

Published by Véhicule Press, Montréal, Québec, Canada
www.vehiculepress.com

Distribution in Canada by LitDistCo
www.litdistco.ca

Distributed in the US by Independent Publishers Group
www.ipgbook.com

Printed in Canada on FSC certified paper.

For Toan, Jesse, and Rachel

CONTENTS

Walking the Dog

Survival Kit

Although the wind
blows terribly here,
the moonlight also leaks
between the roof planks
of this ruined house.

—IZUMI SHIKIBU

Walking the Dog

THE DAYTIME MOON

is at once modest and tenacious,
reflecting the sun's rays while reflecting
upon itself, its tenuous grasp
on our attention.

The way we are startled, seeing it,
then go about our business as though nothing odd
has happened. And it hasn't, for the moon
is always there, even when we don't see it,
the way someone who loves you holds you
in their thoughts,
expectant, tender, patiently holding
and holding
for the moment your thoughts
return to them.

Surely most of us have someone waiting
quietly for us to notice them
waiting quietly?
What will it take for us to turn our gaze
in their direction?
Autumn spends its gold so lavishly you would think
winter has been cancelled, but no,
soon we will huddle inside,
feeling more unloved than ever

while the moon shines on and on.

LIKE INSTRUMENTS

When I was a child
whatever I saw stirred me:
pine cone, seashell, duck, caterpillar,
the sable-tipped russet hairs of a fox,
its golden eyes
full of wilderness,
the wilderness.
Everything was tuned to the same vibration
like instruments to concert A,
despite the momentary dissonance
of red innards by the roadside,
a squirrel's corpse,
grandparents dying one by one,
younger than I am now
though they seemed so old.
Younger than I am now,
grandparents dying one by one,
a squirrel's corpse
of red innards by the roadside.
Despite the momentary dissonance,
like instruments to concert A
everything was tuned to the same vibration—
the wilderness
full of wilderness,
its golden eyes;
the sable-tipped russet hairs of a fox,
pine cone, seashell, duck, caterpillar.
Whatever I saw stirred me
when I was a child.

MAPLE

Perfect September day of high blue sky and sun
on the not-yet-yellow leaves of the Norway maple—
like my people, transplanted from eastern Europe,
like my people, considered by some
invasive.

In its native range, the Norway maple
may live up to 250 years, a good biblical span,
but here, on these cramped city streets,
its roots, lacking space to expand,
may strangle the tree.

Like it or not,
everything is a metaphor for everything else:
fish, virus, star, landmine, tree.

UNUSUALLY WARM FOR NOVEMBER

Death walked into the road
10 o'clock of a Thursday evening.
A woman, youngish, ordinary—
shoulder-length brown hair,
pants, windbreaker—stamped her foot
as though to shoo a cat away,
and I slammed on the brakes
and leaned on the horn,
my heart thumping so
I could not hear the radio, soundtrack
to a heartfelt if jejune depiction
of the random violence of life.

I slammed on the brakes
and she returned to the sidewalk.
She neither sauntered nor fled,
neither sashayed nor skittered,
she simply walked
as though nothing at all had happened,
as though I weren't even there—I
and the stunned driver behind me
who continued up the street at 20 kilometres an hour
four car lengths away,
either fearing proximity to my unfortunate vehicle
or, like me, part of a phantom procession
to the nearest cemetery.

AFTER FINISHING THE CRYPTIC
CROSSWORD, I TOOK THE DOG FOR A WALK

although it had been snowing all day
and did not seem likely to quit
for I knew he loved to rub his black nose
and shaggy ears into fresh drifts
and a dog's joy is not readily discounted.
So we ventured into the world
and discovered a mystery.

At irregular intervals along the sidewalk
bare patches loomed—
something I did not recall having noticed before
and which baffled me
until I realized each one flared from the base of a barren tree
as though it were a memory of that tree's
full-foliaged summer shadow,
the trees themselves stretching generous branches
to the sky, the snow caught up there,
unfallen.

And then, as we rounded the corner,
a single red apple stood, shining, in the road,
bringing to mind the brilliant cardinal
nestled inside a bush on the previous day's walk
who therefore had to fly
into this poem.

At the northwest corner of the park, the white field
was broken, obscenely, by muddy scars
where some heavy vehicle had trundled through
but the tracks stopped, ten metres in,
as though the hand of God had transported
whatever it was skyward,
away from the playground and wading pool,
the basketball and tennis courts.

Soon after, yapping
drew us to the off-leash area
where there was no one,
until the bulky silhouette of a man appeared
at the southeast corner of the park
and my pulse quickened
and I called the dog to go home.
But he was too busy kicking snow to listen
so the fellow caught up to us
and, revealing his smiling boy's face,
bent down to pat the dog.

Shadows that were not shadows.
An apple impersonating a bird.
The boy inside the man.

Mysteries upon mysteries.

THE VIRUS ENTERS THE BODY

The virus enters the body
the way a man enters
a forest:
stealthily.

It is dark in there.
Light filters so faintly
through thick foliage
he cannot discern
what is moving
beyond the trees.

What is moving beyond the trees?
Hostile creatures
or more of his own kind?

He cannot remember
how he arrived at this place
or how long he's been travelling.

He doesn't remember his name
or what his mission is
but he keeps moving because
it gives a shape to his days
and a purpose to his being

and if he dies,
he will at least know that
he died trying—
though trying to go where
or for what reason
is beyond him.

IN QUARANTINE

No hiking the narrow road to the deep north
or the road to Oxiana
no blue highways

no short walks in the Hindu Kush
or in Patagonia
no endurance

no sailing slowly down the Ganges
or to a distant island
no chasing the sea

no travels in the interior of Africa
no travels with a donkey in the Cévennes
no travels with myself and another

no riding the red rooster
no skating to Antarctica
or along the rings of Saturn

no letters from Portugal
no news from Tartary
no notes from a century before

no innocents abroad
whether in the fearful void
or in the impossible country

no roughing it
no time of gifts
no view of the world

WALKING THE DOG

Walking the dog though it's 20 below and neither of us is happy
Salt curdles the ice, scalding his unshod paws

Walking the dog, inspecting the neighbour's gardens
Must ask Ashley for the name of that gold-throated claret lily

Walking the dog to the bank to cheer up the security guard
Who is going stir-crazy watching capitalism's manoeuvres

Walking the dog around the pond where the heron visits
Two painted turtles sun themselves on a log

Walking the dog, inspecting the new crop of babies
Their mothers incandescent with fatigue and with love

Only walking the dog around the block because it's late and I'm tired
The moon shrugs white shoulders and mist diamonds the hedges

Walking the dog at noon when the asphalt, shimmering with heat,
Impersonates water

Walking the dog to the Greek market for feta and olives
Walking the dog to the boulangerie for a baguette

Walking the dog because my mind has stalled
And it is solved by walking

Walking the dog because the news frightens me
Because I need to see trees and he needs to chase some
squirrels

Walking the dog because it is always good
To be walking the dog

A MIND OF WINTER

Reading Elizabeth Bishop in the air
between Montreal and Toronto. Here
is my life, travelling to funerals.
I exaggerate, of course. Sometimes there
are weddings, sometimes births. But it's winter,
the last gasp of a year of death, not life.

Holding this book, I hover over life,
a creature incorporeal as air
or wish I did, as joints complain of winter.
Still, this metal casket suspends me here,
distant from those preoccupied with their
earthbound business. They forget the funeral

that tamps down each day's lid, the funeral
that mocks our frail attempts to varnish life,
the nothing that is always thrumming there—
basso continuo to this mournful air.
Nevertheless, there's something else to hear,
precise, deliberate, cool as winter,

urgent in particulars as winter,
practising love, as at a funeral.
That counter melody insists we're here
to praise beauty, gather wisdom, relish life
under the thin membrane of the air
just by *being*, each being offering their

brief suspension between here and there.
The urgency I feel most in winter
to justify my right to breathe the air
is foolish, a premature funeral.
Every creature is owed a little life,
erratic as is our tenancy here.

That's me pulling up bootstraps you hear,
not entirely persuaded that there's
more purpose for poetry and life
than watching days grow short again in winter,
each year the previous year's funeral.
Still, I breathe the effervescent air

that shouts, "You're here!" My lungs insist on air,
inhale more life even in darkest winter.
(They're doing it now, en route to the funeral.)

THE GLOAMING

A fox in the schoolyard
at twilight, in winter,
whisks his brisk tail, trots
past me and my elderly dog

who cannot see through clouded eyes
his free cousin, cannot scent him
in the frosted air,
doesn't realize what grace

has met us here
now all that is wild recedes
deeper into the past
as though already forgotten.

Twilight defines us;
it is where we live.
The gloaming
in which what glows

is the memory of memory—
a childhood stuffed full
as Noah's ark
with beings we believed

we could save,
those venturing out
almost invisibly
at day's end

to scavenge a few small things
disregarded by us
who, insatiable, consume
whatever we can catch.

Can't catch me!
says Fox,
sauntering into his own
long shadow

ears pricked to hear
all the hidden creatures
still moving
under the moonlit snow.

TO HYPNOS

You always liked to tease me,
waiting patiently until I finished a task
then appearing at the periphery
of my vision, making me chase you
until you caught me in your embrace.
I slipped into it as into a tranquil pool:
cool silk everywhere, no distinction
between our limbs.

Now you sulk in another room,
a disappointed spouse. Nothing I say
appeases you; nothing I do tempts you
to my bed.

How did I offend?
Was it those early mornings in the garden
when I rejoiced to hear the dawn chorus,
those birds who plague you by praising the sun?
Or was it the many midnights
worries wrenched me from your arms
as though your divinity were less worthy
than mortal concerns?

Lord of rest and renewal,
teach me how to regain your love.

LA FLORIDE

Not sand but shells, jagged and unforgiving,
delay our progress to the tepid sea
where brown pelicans dive for fish,
their gullets stuffed full
as picnic hampers.
Ibis venture closer, seeking scraps.

My husband swims laps, tireless,
beyond a line of revellers standing
in the shallows.
They wear straw hats and mirrored glasses
and clutch cokes,
photographing each other's grins
with phones lofted above
the frictionless surf.

The pale shore rolls mildly to the pale water
lapping the pale horizon—
cream to blue-green to blue—
the flag of the country of leisure.

Because it's Sunday
and these good folks deserve
to float under cloudless skies
and do nothing, nothing at all,

while the sea, hot and bothered,
nibbles the beach at their feet,
its appetite as insatiable
as theirs.

JULY AFTERNOON

From his perch in the shadowy cedar,
an enthusiastic robin makes up in volume
what he lacks in melody
while on a bent stalk of dill, a caterpillar,
limber as an acrobat in fluorescent stripes,
obeys his own imperative: to be filled.
After all, who could ever have enough
of summer?

Me, apparently, fallen asleep in my chair.
This heat stupefies; everything shimmers.
In a moment I will finish the book I am reading.
In a moment I will get up and weed the garden.
But first I will listen to the tide of dreams
receding; first I will walk along the shore
where my mind meets my mind
to see what I can find there.

NURSE LOG

Everything is becoming more itself
or something else. A single cedar splits
into seven trunks, one of which is dead.
The others are leafless until twenty feet up
where their green profusion seeks the sky.
Meanwhile the sun infiltrates the forest,
its long fingers stroking the shivering ferns,
the variant silver of lichen and granite,
the gleaming velvet of moss;
red-enamelled mushrooms
shining here and there like flowers.

Smell of growth, smell of decay—
in this place they are the same.

The nurse log sighs and settles deeper into sleep.
Nuzzling into her side a maple sapling
imagines amplitude; beetles burrow
and a red squirrel turns an acorn
in dexterous paws. Above them, invisibly,
the wood thrush pours out her liquid song
of praise, which is the same as her song
of sorrow, which is the same as saying
this is where all things live
and all things die

and all things are reborn.

HER PAST

comes to her like flickers
of crimson koi,
water lilies wavering
amid reflected clouds

except those would not be her images.
She sees childish toes, feels them dig
into warm dirt—
her aunt's goose farm, white feathers
aloft in the air like snow

or like spume behind the boat
bearing her to America:
to the father who had found safety
in another life, another language.

After she had forgotten most of that second life,
she still remembered the first,
spoke the words "Mama" and "Papa"
with a Yiddish accent

and described how she and her sister
saved each scant nickel
to go to the movies in the shtetl

but in the shtetl
there were neither nickels nor movies,
so that must have happened in New York.

"Mama" and "Papa," she crooned,
as if repeating beloved names
would bring their bearers back.
"Vishtinitz," she sang, and "New York."

My own parents never got old enough
to forget the past,
though the pain of cancer erased all else
those last terrible weeks.

Even us, their children, waiting
to receive their blessings:
blessings which never came.

Which is worse, I wonder:
To grasp at a chorus of ghosts receding
or to be trapped in a present of meaningless pain?
And what do people mean
when they speak of "a good death"?

MINDFUL

What I miss about him is a stillness he inhabited
or, to be accurate, mostly just pursued
by going fishing or listening to Bach,
holding his right hand up, palm out,
to request quiet in that house full of too much
of everything: people, noise, obligations.

The way he closed his eyes
to make it all go away.

He did this instinctively, the *abhaya mudra*,
Buddha's gesture of blessing or protection.
Whenever I need reassurance,
I remember him conducting silence
and enter that silence.

What I miss about her is that absurd intensity
which exhausted everyone with its insistence
that everything be the most, the best, always.
That anything less was failure.
Not because this was a good way to live,
because it sure as hell wasn't

but because it was a useful reminder
to try to leave things better
than we found them.

Stillness and striving,
my fraught tormented parents,
then and now.

EMPORIUM

When summer came, we made a pilgrimage across the border
to Gaynes Shoppers World, Mecca to Montrealers,
packed to the ceiling with Levi's denim overalls,
Bass Weejuns penny loafers, Nancy Drew mysteries
and Clark's Teaberry gum, five pieces for 7 cents.

All the stuff needed to escape censure at school:
the stuff that would make us cool.

American ingenuity was inexhaustible, unlike our budget.
We had to leave so much behind—
patio furniture and portable record players,
ten-speed Osterizer Pulse-Matic blenders
and Charmglow Party Host barbecue grills.

My father settled for fishing lures, drill bits,
and barbecue-flavoured chips;
he pulled his flat dad-wallet out of his back pocket,
gassed up the car and drove home, feeling munificent.
That's what dads did in those days.

But at customs he went undercover, lying to the border guards
whose Ray-Bans scrutinized us squirming in the back seat,
each wearing two pairs of jeans and three T-shirts,
lumber jackets chafing our necks
where price tags had been raggedly snipped off.

He waved around a bag of tube socks and PJs,
a few packs of Teaberry gum.
"Can't get that in Canada, can you?" the guards said,
as though it made perfect sense to drive all the way to Vermont
just to buy gum.

And he would nod back, knowing that they knew but didn't care,
that we all had more, so much more, to declare.

Survival Kit

ONION

I am sorry that I made you cry. It was not my intention; it never is. Yet whenever I let someone get close to me, this is what happens. Because I hold myself so tightly, shielding this thin skin from the world's lacerations.

But what exactly am I protecting? I no longer remember. My secrets are so profoundly hidden even I cannot hear them whisper.

Because I refuse to remember the past, each successive moment shrouds me with another layer of loss. I know that this makes me look old, and even wise, to those who, like you, study my countenance for what it seems to reveal about life. You believe what you see. But don't. The lines that endurance has engraved on this face are proof of nothing except time. Time that makes us all weep, in the end.

LETTUCE

They say I'm frivolous, a frill, a can-can dancer, a chancer;
they say I'm all talk and no action. They say I'm 95% water,
wavering and green, a dizzy queen boasting of her salad days,
dazed. They say I've got no insides inside, nothing but air
there; that I'm all flourish, unable to nourish.

Let us consider the facts. I may be mostly water but so are you.
And if water were a vegetable, it would look like me, billow
after billow, at once moving and contained. Rhythm sustained.
A stationary fish. A wish. A wave as thin as a blade. Mermaid.

Solid rain, I must be devoured fresh; I cannot be baked or
fried, frozen or dried. I am purely myself, the smallest leaf a
true copy of the largest, a series of herbaceous echoes. Fling
each layer aside—I've nothing to hide. It's all me, all the way
through. I'm true.

They say I taste of nothing, but that is because they have
burnt their tongues on bitter fare and I savour of spring: its
cool nights, its dew-bespangled dawns. Like a new-laid lawn,
I am full of expectation, regeneration.

Let me lay my cool wrists on your fevered cheeks.

TOMATO

The ancient Aztecs described me as "fat water with a navel" and Swedish botanist Carl Linnaeus as a "wolfpeach." That is, I was seen as a chimera long before a flounder's gene was injected into my rump. Even today, you can't decide whether I am fruit or vegetable, salad or dessert—whether I am the cause of your bodily inflammation or its potential cure.

This is how you assess everyone you meet, whether they extend an open hand or a mailed fist, invite you for dinner or chase you out of town with flaming torches. Among comrades, aquiver with mistrust, you question whether they are virtuous or wicked, doomed or saved. Because you wonder that about yourself. The culpability of your own actions a dagger to the heart.

But I am here for a good time, not a long time. Summer tastes best fresh off the sun-ripened vine, eaten with a sprinkle of salt or a splash of balsamic vinegar. I am a creature of infinite variety: chutney, salsa, gazpacho; caprese, confit, shakshuka; marinara, ratatouille, tabbouleh. I put the *pizzazz* in pizza, the *mmmmmmah* in your mouth.

I would say, "Lighten up!" I would exhort you to "be here now" or ask, "If not now, when?" if I thought you would listen. O, let your dear heart recognize mine, so round and sweet, so full of elation at the mystery of things! But I know that is not your nature. Taking things easy is just too difficult for you.

POTATOES

Rosary of the earth, we have always tried to keep you safe. Holding hands through the ages, all the way back to the Mesozoic, forming a chain to tow you out of famine. An heirloom necklace of pearls. A sympathetic smile with no menace in its teeth.

You are easily seduced by our more glamorous cousins—the vivacious tomato, sleepy nightshade, mystical tobacco—but we are the ones you come home to. Roam where you must, voyager; you will always find us awaiting your return. Asleep under a spray of flowers, pillowed deep into the soil. We ask so little in recompense: a warm bed, the occasional shower of rain. And our generosity is legendary! We answer your care tenfold.

You call us "humble," as though humility is somehow regrettable, but we regret nothing and never have. We know exactly who we are and why we are here. How many creatures are as resolutely themselves? How many live only to succour others?

How many have done so for eons, without pretence or prevarication?

A necklace of pearls. A chain to tow you out of famine.

Rosary of the earth.

APPLE

You have never trusted my innocent demeanour, suspecting these rosy cheeks were flushed not with modesty but with guilt. The Greeks blamed me for the Trojan War, the Jews for the Fall of Man, Scandinavians for threatening the immortality of the very gods themselves. But what did I do to merit such suspicion? My blossoms are delicate and fair, smelling of zephyrs and possibility. My fruit, whether tart or sweet, is both delicious and medicinal. Fermented, I yield a cider that has sustained thousands through times of suspect water and inadequate food. Why, then, am I a symbol of discord rather than harmony? Why am I so often coupled with a snake?

These are the mysteries I ponder through the short summer nights as the moon, my celestial twin, waxes and wanes. We smile at each other across space and time, retelling the ancient tales. For she was there, the glimmering girl with flowers in her hair, *la Bella Luna*. She was there and heard every plucked lyre of every stammering bard: solitary, hovering, fruit of an invisible tree. The silver apple who never falls to earth.

Cathedral/Grove

where are those voices coming from
        voices of praise
                voices of lamentation

They are coming from under the earth
from the fallen altars of Tarvos and Esus
Smertrios and Cernunnos

the old gods of this island
upon whose sacred ground
the Romans built a temple to Jupiter

their angry Skyfather
to whom we also knelt
hoping to appease the conquerors

in their helmets of shining metal
cuirasses of shining metal
trampling our sacred island

forbidden to return home without conquest
men who killed our children
because they could not embrace their own

We sacrificed to the Roman deities
hoping not for divine favour
—it was too late for divine favour—

but that if we respected their
rapacious gods
they might allow us to keep ours

voices under the earth
        where the river of gold runs deep

∾

Gold our smiths fashioned for hundreds of years
into torcs we hung from our necks
and wound round the arms of our children

human art channelling the power of the gods
energy leaping across the gap in the torc
from one side to the other like lightning

golden lightning above the marshes
during summer storms, lightning
that split the great oaks of the sacred grove

lightning golden as the metal
the Romans craved
and for which they killed our people

our people down there, under the earth
        singing the ancient songs
                of praise
                        and lamentation

∾

Light a torch, carve steps down
into darkness; a slight phosphorescence
will show you where to go

you can see it best out of the corner of your eye
if you don't focus too keenly
that is how to find all the bright things

meteors
  jewels
    the shades of our vanquished people

Follow them as they followed Vercingetorix
he of the beautiful horses
master of strategy

whose true name we never revealed
to the Romans, just as we hid from them
the true nature of our gods

Follow them as we followed him
against all odds
against the unquenchable armies of Caesar

with their blood-red shields
their helmets flaunting
blood-red feathers

∾

We also lit torches in those days
burning our settlements
behind us

destroying with heavy hearts
all that we had built
so the Romans would inherit nothing

but still our defences failed
our tribes were too scattered across Gaul
too unused to collaboration

to oppose an empire
for we were not an empire
we were just a people

the Parisii
a few people on the banks
of the river

hedged in by marshes where the Druids gathered
hundreds of years after the Romans
profaned our altars

to the gods they never knew
the true gods of this place
gone down under the earth

> *still singing the ancient songs*
> *of praise*
> *and lamentation*

❧

We lived peacefully on the island
far-famed as sailors and fishermen
grew just what we needed for ourselves

were not ambitious to cover the earth
with our banners
kept our offspring close

meteors
       jewels

The Romans contrived to ship our abundance
elsewhere
mostly home to their masters

timber, grain, beer, iron, wine, slaves, timber
always more timber
their own forests gone under the axe

They cut down trees to clear land
for their soldiers
soldiers who never went home again

some of them had no home
having been swept up by the Roman army
as it ravaged the world

some of them had no families
having enlisted as youths
seeking glory only in battle

> *the shades of our vanquished people*
> *still singing*
> *under the earth*

      ∾

They walled in our island
and renamed it Lutetia
meaning "place near a swamp"

built straight roads to march on
with their straight legs
carrying their straight spears

our sacred oaks
hundreds of years old
they cut for timber

everywhere they went
the land burned
and the Druids wept

> *still singing the ancient songs*
> *of praise*
> *and lamentation*

∾

until the Franks brought a new religion
with a new god
who came back from the dead

a god praised for mercy
though his priests showed us
no mercy

and Jupiter's temple
was torn down
its marble columns plundered

to build a church to Saint Étienne
a man honoured for martyrdom
strange to pray to someone who died

and was not reborn
stranger still to replace the Skyfather
with a mere mortal

The Druids laughed
as did the true gods of this place
to whom we had in times of famine offered

human sacrifice
that the rain might fall
and the harvest flourish

gods we knew to be fierce and unpredictable
as life itself
is fierce and unpredictable

> *voices from under the earth*
>> *where the river of gold runs deep*

∾

Soon two more churches were built
one dedicated to God's mother
the Romans would have called her Hera

but Hera was not a virgin
that was Athena Parthenos
whose body was unmarked by childbirth

Like the Roman faith
this new religion demanded
we believe in things

no man had ever seen
and worship an ever-increasing number of gods
that they called "saints"

maybe we should have made a saint
of Vercingetorix
who martyred himself to save his people

though his sacrifice failed
for the Romans showed us
no mercy

> *the shades of our vanquished people*
> *still singing*
> *under the earth*

∾

Then the Vikings came upon us
like lightning above the marshes
lightning that split the great oaks

of the sacred grove
Four times they returned
not even the plague

could drive them away
only a fortune in gold
stopped the slaughter

but still they sacked the city
destroying all that they touched
including the Virgin's church

though it was soon rebuilt
unlike the greenwood burning burning
burned to the ground

> *still singing the ancient songs*
> *of praise*
> *and lamentation*

∾

Though the Romans were defeated
and the Vikings went home
our people remained captive

their labour belonging to those
who owned the land
Mothers and infants too often died

meteors
> *jewels*

so they preferred the gentle virgin
to any other god
and her cult grew

and the church of Saint Étienne was demolished
as the Temple of Jupiter had been
to make way for a more glorious cathedral

Five generations laboured
to fulfill Bishop de Sully's dream
of vaults, naves, transepts, and choirs

five generations of masons
and brick layers
and stone carvers

before the sculptors and glass makers
turned the building
into a book for the unlettered

ᕲ

When axes toppled the last of our sacred oaks
relics of the forests of Cernunnus
the horned god

> *of praise*
> *and lamentation*

the greenwood that had echoed with the wild hunt
and provided shade and succour to every living thing
vanished

and in its stead men built an artificial heaven
drawing the eye up and up
into a sky of stone

to imitate sunlight through trees
they made windows of glass
and for many years the poor sought solace there

until the revolution came
and they found in their marrow the strength
of Vercingetorix

> *still singing the ancient songs*

and rejected those who promised they would be rewarded
for obedience
only after death

❧

They decapitated the statues of kings
as they decapitated those kings
themselves

but their sacrifice failed
as had that of Vercingetorix
he of the beautiful horses

and the kings came back
and the church prevailed
and again, the Druids wept

as they still weep
for finally a great fire came
like lightning out of the sky

golden lightning over the marshes
and not only our sacred grove
was lost

but even the last oaks plundered from it
were lost
and shall never be found again

> *the shades of our vanquished people*
> *still singing*
> *under the earth*

Survival Kit

KNIFE

I have always been your lucky talisman, warm in your hand.
It was I who nudged you beyond necessity and taught you to
make or break the world. Before me, the world was a predator
and you were the trembling prey. With me in charge, the prey
was ours. Our enemies grew fearful when they saw us coming;
small animals scattered. We hunted and then we feasted; we
stripped sinews to set bowed instruments singing.

You might not remember, but I do. I remember everything.

I remember scratching pictures on the walls of caves as you
sang and prayed to your gods. I remember scraping hides to
make garments, cutting thread to decorate them with beads.
I remember cleaning broken nails and shaping ragged hair;
I remember cutting umbilical cords and hearing babies cry
out in the bright air.

Together we made wounds and cleaned them, scaled fish and
disembowelled caribou. I remember pulling out their sharp
bones. I remember being sharp bone.

I remember everything.

You've known me longer than you've known fire; without me, you would have lacked fuel and that fire would have gone out. But you forget. You forget how much you owe to me. Distracted, you toss me in a drawer with newer tools whose jobs I once did all by myself. Is that why you have forgotten my true nature? Because now you have so many shiny toys?

Do not forget my true nature. I remember everything, and my resentment is as sharp as my memory. If you do not hold me right, I will bite.

SECATEURS

The collective is always more important than the individual, however brilliant that individual might be. Bees know this. Ants know this. If you don't know this, you know nothing.

What I offer is not punishment but freedom. The space between bodies is what allows them to move. It is what allows them to breathe. Think of my work, then, as a form of choreography. Or perhaps you prefer a different metaphor? Like an editor, I tease out hidden stories. Like a sculptor, I carve away excess, uncovering the truth.

Because truth is beauty. In the garden anyway, if not universally. I won't argue that the equation holds everywhere because my jurisdiction is confined to this fragrant patch of earth. But where else would I want to be? From the first tentative ferns to the arrogance of roses, from the sky-mirroring delphiniums to the bee-busy monarda. Such infinite variety! No other realm could satisfy me better or draw from me more tenderness and care.

Yes, I stake a claim for tenderness. I am all tempered steel, my blades so elegantly calibrated that they do not damage buds below the lopped-off stems. In other words, there is no cruelty in my caress. Is the wind cruel for tumbling the peony at its peak of sweetness? Is the rain cruel because it spills petals across the flagstones like tears? What of the ravenous caterpillar, making lace of leaves to feed his metamorphosis, or the lily beetle, that scarlet imp, destroying blossoms that might have challenged her own brightness?

What is the garden but a sequence of exquisite moments en route to an unknown future? What do I do but serve the garden, teasing randomness into form so that my vision of perfection may be savoured in its inevitable passing?

FILE

"American Pattern files are available in three grades of cut: Bastard, Second Cut, and Smooth."
    –KMS Tools File Identification Chart

Don't call me a bastard! Think of me as the ocean, speeded up. If I could tumble you in my arms for years, whispering sweet nothings, I would. My intentions are that pure. But we have so little time, my darling, and you demand perfection. It is your own vanity that makes you put yourself in my rough hands. I could love you the way you are, but you insist on self-improvement.

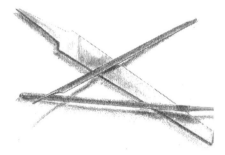

It isn't easy being rough when my only goal is softness. If I could wear away my own barbs I would, believe me. That's the paradox that blackens my heart, and everyone's: what appears a flaw is also a gift. My defect is the same as my excellence. It's Shakespearean, really. Think of Othello or Hamlet: what makes them great is the same quality that defeats them.

I am incapable of dissemblance in a world that expects glib charm. Remember: to "defile" something is to corrupt or stain it; "undefiled" means "chaste." Un + de = two negatives that make a positive. The positive is my heart, as steady as the ocean and that pure.

CLAMP

The emptiness of my arms appalls me, so I wrap them around myself. I wrap myself with my empty arms but it does no good. I shake and shake and can never get warm, though for months my arms ached with his weight and the sweat ran down my brow and I had no free hand to wipe it away. For months we walked through mountain passes wary of snakes and through dusty fields where insects stung; along racing rivers too dangerous to cross and beside roads full of oblivious traffic; in and out of villages: hungry, thirsty, and frightened, surviving on a few coins and the generosity of strangers almost as poor as ourselves. We walked on and walked on and though we were scared, I carried all my hopes in my arms—arms that were never empty. He held on tight, my sweet, sweet child! He held on so tightly I couldn't tell where he ended and I began.

And now my arms are empty and I have no more hope. I have had no hope since we reached the border where they stole my child from me. It took three big men to separate us, we were clamped so tightly together. I thought they would surely kill him—he was so small and their hands were cleavers and their eyes held no tenderness. They were hurting my darling, and I thought I would die. And maybe I did die, for I have no life now that my arms are empty.

HAMMER

He cannot remember ever having been small, though he must have been, once. Surely he was once as slim as the boys under his command? So many boys, lithe and laughing, eager for employment. They arouse uncomfortable feelings in him, feelings he avoids by shouting. He repeats himself, repeats himself, repeats himself, to get the job done. He is a true believer; no one is more dedicated. No one stands straighter or hits harder.

He always says, "This is going to hurt me more than it hurts you." But since the boys have never seen him cry, they don't believe him. He never mentions the word "sacrifice," though he leaves their bodies at the front each night and goes home alone, his head ringing.

Chimera

אייערלעך

The dream of the house with hidden rooms
that I only remember in the midst of the dream of the house
with hidden rooms. The dreams nested inside each other
like matryoshka dolls, the ones my grandmother gave me
that I entrusted to my own daughter
so the generations are sheltered inside one another
like hidden rooms in the dream of the house
with hidden rooms.

When I was young, one might cut open a chicken
and find an unhatched egg inside her. Those were the days.
Vasily Zvyozdochkin carved the first matryoshka doll
in Russia in the 1890s. It represented eight generations.
I can only go back three, my great-grandparents
having fled pogroms in Russia in 1881
and 1888. There are no records, no stories,
not even rumours about my family before they left.
Hidden rooms in the dream of the house with hidden
rooms.

THE SMELL OF SMOKE

> "now stroke your strings then as smoke
> you will rise into air"
>
> > – "Death Fugue," translated
> > by Michael Hamburger

I can only go back three generations
on both sides of   my family my
    great-grandparents having fled
the pogroms or   conscription into
    the Tsar's armies to burn down
Jewish villages   they were
    fleeing the smell of smoke

Those are the stories I have
on both sides   of my family
    my father as a child in Montreal
sleeping   under his bed
    so the Cossacks couldn't find him
He grew up   went to university
    still fleeing the smell of smoke

So the Cossacks couldn't find
and punish   their families
    the refugees gave false addresses
thousands of Jews   from who knows where
    claiming to have come from the same
mythical village   They were all
    fleeing the smell of smoke

        after the assassination of the Tsar
on his way home   to the Winter Palace
        from the Mikhailovsky Manège
where once   a lonely elephant sheltered
        Alexander Nikolaevich Romanov
survived the first bomb   but succumbed to the second
        while fleeing the smell of smoke

        He liberated the serfs 68 years after
Upper Canada   outlawed slavery
        but he did not emancipate the Jews
who were blamed   for his death
        though he had been murdered by Russian anarchists
259 pogroms followed   leaving my people
        fleeing the smell of smoke

        which is why I don't know
where it was   they came from
        or even who my ancestors were
Better to be nobody   from nowhere
        no records no stories not even
rumours   about my family
        Nothing more than the smell of smoke

AKEDAH

Growing up in Quebec
I didn't understand
why the tortured man

hung writhing in every public building
or why, if he was supposed to be God's son,
God would let people kill him

or how he could be God himself
because everyone knows that gods
can't die.

My later devotion to Western culture
compelled me to lock such questions away
where only occasionally my eye fell on them

as on the butchered carcass
from which the aromatic roast
ensued.

It was impossible to savour English Lit
without accepting its myths

though I was told they were "truths"
which the sacred texts of my own people
had merely "adumbrated."

Such grand Latin to hide the insult—
one of many to which I turned the other cheek
as professor after professor made excuses

for centuries of anti-Semitism
as an outmoded perspective
we had to accept

and even excuse
because of its historical context
and the acute understanding of human character

and elegant compositions of those who espoused it
in our *Norton Anthology* of the discipline's
greatest hits.

Nor were we to question their contention
that the "Old" Testament deity was a god of Judgment
while the "New" Testament version was a god of Love.

A conundrum when you think about it
—as you were not meant to—
because the Torah

rejects human sacrifice, freeing Isaac,
but the Christian bible requires it.

Even if we browsed *The Golden Bough*
and learned that Osiris, Tammuz, Adonis,
Attis, and Dionysus

all died and were resurrected,
we were not supposed to notice how this trope
functions in our own culture

or, more accurately, the culture
we were allowed to pretend was ours
as long as we didn't ask impertinent questions.

I swallowed my tongue so often
it's amazing I can still speak.

What's most striking about the *akedah*
is not that Isaac escaped being sacrificed
but that father Abraham

slunk off covertly
with his knife and his bundle of wood
without informing Sarah.

He knew she would not allow it.
What mother would?

Sarah is only mentioned a few pages later
when she dies and is buried at Kiryat Arba
betrayed and perhaps bitter

but not weeping over the marble corpse
of her son.
She was spared that, at least,

though like Mary she knew
he was the child of God.
Because every child is.

HINENI

An eye studies a slide to locate the single vector of infection.
A shepherd counts sheep obscured by snow.
A mother runs frantic through the playground
searching for her lost child.

"Where are you?" each calls, silently or aloud,
hoping for "Here I am!" in response.

But why would God need to ask? I used to wonder,
imagining an obdurate patriarch peering
from the sky, penetrating all places at once,
hearing my every thought
and judging my every deed.

178 times in the Torah the question is posed.
More uncertainty there
than is ever acknowledged, the creator
having lost track of his creatures
and doubting their devotion.

What if Abraham kept shtum or Moses
clamped his jaw shut? What if they refused to be chosen
and detoured into ordinary life?
Sadie and Abe growing old together
as their flocks flourish and their grandkids
tumble at their feet. Moishe
a prince of Egypt, his tongue unscathed by fire,
his eyes outlined in kohl.

THE MERMAID OF ZENNOR

Though the echoing spaces of Europe's cathedrals
have always impressed me
more as evidence of humanity's lonely hopes
than the certitude of its faith,

they still buzz with surprising power:
gothic generators storing energy
quarried from rock and hammered from bronze
wrought with sweat and burning muscles

filtering through stained glass
like the sun's rays through oak and cedar
like the sun's rays through water
like the sun's rays through fingers splayed

in front of eyes clenched shut in terror
before that first of the gods
whose glory all people acknowledge
without whom there is only darkness and cold

without whom we could not have found our way
out of the infinite forests
that everywhere surrounded us
into the vexed present where the forests

are gone. The forests are gone, and you too
are gone, my dear friend, like the mermaid
of Zennor, down under the sea with her haunting voice
still singing in our memories.

I wish I could be with you again at Saint Senara
within the sound of the sea and the mermaid's voice;
I would worship with you at Saint Senara
on that gorse-covered coast

or in one of those Greek chapels one stumbles upon
on some bare hilltop where only a donkey grazes
the scrubby, heat-baked soil under a cloudless sky
and the custodian's creased face lights up

at the prospect of a visitor. In such places
it is still possible to pray.

CHIMERA

"Here a horrible ghoul looks at you, a bear with ass's ears,
a horned cow, a frighteningly lascivious goat, a phantom
leaving the coffin, and the most damned of all, a Jew with
his pointed cap."

–Auguste-Marc Bayeux,
"La Flèche de Notre-Dame," 1860

Some call me "The Alchemist" because of my cap
and flowing beard

others assume I am the "mischievous portrait"
of "a demanding taskmaster"

made by a disgruntled stonemason
working under Viollet-le-Duc

god of this Olympus
father of gargoyles and chimeras

custodian of superstition and enabler
of the superstitious.

But who I represent is, in fact, quite clear:
Le Juif errant, that medieval bogeyman

condemned to roam the earth forever
because he mocked the Christian god.

You will not find me in the bible
so don't lick your finger to turn the page.

Doubting Thomas is there but he was forgiven
because eventually he believed

as those who remained observant Jews
did not.

Their descendants are still waiting
for the Messiah

or at least for the messianic age
which seems as far away as ever

if not farther. Our distance from paradise
may be precisely why my image

is not grotesque: despite himself
Viollet-le-Duc sympathized

with my idealism—that thwarted hope
for a better world some day.

I am no monster but fully human.
Old and sad perhaps

as you too will be old and sad one day
though, unlike me, you will be granted rest

while my legend keeps wandering the weary ages
travelling as easily among the infected

as any other plague.

WHAT I LEARNED FROM LIVING ABROAD

Wherever you go, locals love their place best
and assume you are visiting because your homeland is inferior

or you couldn't find a husband there
or occasionally both. This leads to some awkward conversations

but switching from politics and sex to the topic of food
guarantees a happier exchange.

Admiring babies is non-controversial
but do not pat their round heads or squeeze their chubby toes

without permission. The same goes for dogs
though folks are less indignant

if you cannot refrain from embracing their pets.
Whenever you enter a place of worship

cover your head and shut your mouth.
Remember how few of us have encountered a deity

and respect the attempts of so many to commune with one
even in places that represent the acquisition of wealth

through the oppression of citizens or by means of imperial conquest.
Having lit a candle to honour your own persecuted ancestors

return to the topic of food or, failing that,
sit at a café table and sketch your surroundings.

People are offended when you take a photo without asking
but delighted when you draw them—

everyone wants to ascend, so when prayer fails,
art will serve.

COLOUR THEORY

Like most ancient civilizations, the Greeks
had no word for blue.
Did they fail to perceive it
or was it too obvious to require naming?
Just everywhere, like the air.

Thus Homer's "wine-dark" sea was not
Mediterranean turquoise
but other, turbulent,
driven by God-breath and fate:
οἶνοψ πόντος, the element heroes sail on.

Although he also described sheep as "wine-coloured"
so what do I know?

I know this: all blues are cool
but some blues are cooler.
For $100 a litre
you can buy a tin of Klein blue

approximating the hue the artist copyrighted
before his death at 34.
It will cover 85 square feet at $1.17647058824
per square foot; 2.5 square feet for every year
of his brief life.

And now I am thinking that nobody has square feet
just like nobody has white skin.
Or black skin for that matter.
Though there are green-faced men in Homer
and in the comic books of my youth, some of whom

had eyes resembling ping-pong balls on stalks
much like the stomapods, also known as
mantis shrimp who, of all earthly creatures,
have the best sense of sight.

How drunk they must be
in their wine-dark sea
fathoming all those blues!

TRYING TO REREAD THE *ILIAD* IN 2020

I.

My old dog whimpers in sleep, blind paws scrabbling
the air. Who knows whether he is chased or chases,
whether it is the same dream each night or many?
Docile all day, dormant the wolf revives. The hunt
is never so far down he cannot retrieve it.

We are no better, obsessed with Troy's fall as though
it can explain us to ourselves in finer language.

II.

I'd grown so tired of Canadian poets
strip-mining Homer to add gravitas to their works
I vowed I'd never do it. But here I am,
wondering if there's anything more to learn peering
through the rear-view mirror as the future careens
away, a question mark on a digital screen
on a spacecraft seeking a habitable planet:

that is, a rock not too far off with oxygen
and water, some decorative greenery and
no predators, reptilian or otherwise.
But will we recognize them if they're there?
No one meeting us would know we were evil, would they?

I began this poem contemplating my dog, who
thinks I am good. But once on a hike, I scooped up
a wee toad and put him in a plastic container
to study later before releasing. I forgot
he was there, and he died.

III.

Lessons from Homer: once engaged in battle,
men are compelled to continue because withdrawing
without winning is too shameful. Also: prowess
in fighting is no guarantee of victory
if the capricious gods are not on your side. And
news flash: women are trophies without agency.

The moments of the poem I like best abandon
the war, its non-stop amputation of heads and hands
as though armoured men are delicatessen fare,
some fat, some lean, some bloodier than others, all
spouting their lineage as they go down to the earth.

It's boring. But there is so much of it you can't
just skip the carnage. Words absent from the *Iliad*:
"hoe"
    "pitcher"
        "nephew"
            "daydream"
                "joke"
                    "happiness"
                        "pet."

IV.

Against the spectacle of war and the tantrums
of Olympus abides the daily life of beasts.
Nature perpetually *there*, outside the frame,
assurance that life itself will still continue
day and night, winter and summer, undying
no matter what grief men act upon each other.

If only that were true! Lifting up the corner
of the canvas, we find no pastoral idyll
but flood and fire, forests clear-cut, habitats
killed by successive generations, each proclaiming
its righteous cause, each stuffed full of lies and bravado
like those foolish Greeks and their equally foolish gods.

v.

Some Species Extinct in Greece and Asia Minor
since Homer's Time

Asiatic lions
Aurochs
Tarpans
The Arabian ostrich
The Caspian tiger
The Anatolian leopard
The Caucasian elk
The Caucasian bison
The Eurasian beaver
The Cyprus dipper
The heavenly fish

VI.

O Cyprus dipper! O Caspian tiger! O
heavenly fish! I wish you an eternity
of clean water and no hunters whose vanity
demands your death, just the incidental dangers
we all face, being alive. But of course, you aren't.

Neither are they, those heroes lauded by Homer.
There's less proof of their existence than of yours;
less than that of the toad I plucked from his green world
and killed. Another paradox: that negligence
can make one just as guilty as outright malice.

VII.

The word "negligence" cannot be found in the *Iliad* either.

AQUARIUM

A week or two each August for nine years,
we lived our heart's desire, surrounded by water
and birdsong and starlight;
pulled on bathing suits in the morning
and stripped them off reluctantly at night

when we emptied the aquarium
filled daily with creatures aquatic or terrestrial,
best of all a tree frog whose gelatinous toes,
splayed out on the tank's sheer walls,
hoisted him up to its artificial heaven.

Our children were small, then bigger; outgrowing
the glistening sunfish they reeled in off the dock,
evenings playing Scrabble or watching meteors scatter.
They became restless, requiring frequent trips to town
where they checked their email at the library

and browsed stores for frivolous cargo:
T-shirts with silly slogans, exploding candy.
Soon friends bussed up north to join them
in secretive conversations on the dock,
late nights watching movies on their laptops.

Eventually the cottage failed to contain them.
We could no longer spy on their antics.
Summers are long now in the hot city,
waiting for them to email us from
wherever they go to next.

SPRING

Monochrome day, gunmetal sky,
streets streaked with dirty snow
when from the top of a leafless maple
a cardinal whoops.
"I am red! he cries, "I am
red, redder, reddest!"
before dropping down one branch
to bounce into emptiness,
a diver on the high board.

In his wake
my vision's sharper.
How did I not notice buds
poised to burst at twig tip,
green beaks chipping
at the thawing soil?

FRASS

Absorbed in deadheading roses
peonies and day lilies
weeding between the ruffled heads
of lettuce, the toppled rhubarb stalks

pinching back tomato plants
pruning stray branches
to let sunlight brighten
the garden

I ignored an infestation
of sawfly larvae
on the not-yet-blooming loosestrife
until they had made ribbons

of the leaves. Isn't that how it always is?
Problems multiply unnoticed
in the lea of our preoccupations
until they have grown riotous.

It's not that the insects hadn't left signs—
tiny balls of excrement marking their journey—
but that I hadn't focused
close enough to see them

until I did, and then the trail
was everywhere
as were the silvery greenish creatures
curled peacefully under the leaves.

Almost phosphorescent, they were
beautiful in their own way
and might have become more so
had I let them live to see

their wings unfold—
had I let them become themselves.

But I didn't.

DAPHNE AND APOLLO

In Ovid's *Metamorphoses*,
women fleeing the lust
of importunate gods and godlings
are sometimes transformed into trees,

their perception of time
slowing down during a crisis
becomes embodied—
feet affix to soil, roots dig deep,
arms yearn skyward,
bark creeps over mouths
panting in terror.

Let us hope, over time,
memory fades.
Insects bustle up and down trunks
whose heartbeat has slowed,
songbirds perch on fingers,
squirrels chatter,
and all creatures shelter from rain or sun
below kindly branches.

To become a tree is,
after all, not the worst fate
one can imagine.

At El Bosque Tallado
in El Bolsón, Argentina,

the remains of lenga beech
left by two forest fires
have been carved into people,
sinuous or whimsical,
playful or solemn,
by artists reluctant to let the burned stumps
symbolize nothing but ruin.

For those trees perhaps
becoming human was a form of redemption.
(As for Apollo, he never changed.
That's what being a god means.)

THE PERSEIDS

I'm sitting in my ergonomic chair watching rain
draw exclamation marks against the window.
If I were at a cottage I could go for a swim—
water meeting water at the lake—

or build a lean-to of fallen branches and driftwood,
roof it with boughs of fragrant cedar,
spread a tarpaulin to keep my sleeping bag dry
and read by flashlight until the clouds slipped away
and the moon's scimitar skimmed the black ripples

at which time I would sit on the dock
and drink starlight, waiting for the Perseids
to fling themselves headlong
across the sky. Silly girls,
August makes them so reckless!

THE GREENWOOD

> "I kan noght parfitly my Paternoster as the preest it syngeth,
> But I kan rymes of Robyn Hood."
>
> –William Langland, *The Vision of Piers Plowman*, c. 1370

Who is more beguiling than Robin Hood
to any child or outcast?
Living in the forest with a family
of his own choosing,
making fires and shooting arrows,
robbing the rich to feed the poor,
at once hero and villain, beyond
all social norms—

that is to say, absolutely free.

I loved him with an ardour
that was pure romance. Not exactly sexless—
for I had an idea that kissing was part of it
and was jealous of Maid Marian—
but mostly out of body. The soul's aspiration
for a world of justice and simplicity

as in the summer
when we rented a cottage
and I could spend all day outdoors
alone, climbing trees, picking berries,
finding the brightest stone
in the cold, cold lake
for my collection.

So when I met a man from Nottingham,
it was ordained we should fall in love
and our relationship should be doomed.

A story for another day, or maybe never.

What I remember best about Sherwood Forest
is a wall of rhododendrons taller than me,
but memory, as usual, is capricious.
That brilliant hedge did not surround the forest
but a nearby park, tamed and planted
as Robin Hood himself has been
by local entrepreneurs.
You can have the Robin Hood Experience
or take the Robin Hood Tour, drink ale
at the Robin Hood pub.
You can visit the thousand-year-old "Major Oak,"
which won Tree of the Year in 2014—
a tree older than the hooded man himself,
already rooted when Nottingham Castle was built
and when the oldest pub in the country,
"Ye Olde Trip to Jerusalem,"
poured its first pints

and when the Jews of Nottingham
were slaughtered during the Second Barons' War.

The legend of Robin Hood first appears
during the reign of those French-speaking barons
at whose tables Saxon "sheep" became Norman *mouton*,
Saxon "swine" *porc*, Saxon "cows" *boeuf*;
who barred the Saxon peasantry, on pain of death,

from hunting in the greenwood
where Saxon "deer" became Norman *venison*

though the deer themselves
were neither Norman nor Saxon
but a golden river under the green trees
of the greenwood, their antlers
another kind of forest, moving.

GREEN TOMATOES

The weather forecast
calls for frost

so I picked the green tomatoes
to make salsa and chutney,
plucked the last of the basil for pesto,

fragrances transporting me
to Mexico, India, and Italy—
places I once travelled
but have little hope of seeing again.

Are these the last days?

As I store each jar
against the coming dark
when we shall all be shut in
in fear of each other,
in fear of our very breath,
the question hovers in the air,
more pungent than those odours
that briefly gave me comfort.

My children are all I care about now.
Oh, whatever powers there are,
please let what is still green
ripen in the sun
as it should.

AFTER PASTERNAK

A man walking through fields at turn of season
forgets his life:
what he says about it when his feet are squared under a table
and everyone's talking too fast,
or how he lines up those memories by his bed each night
like shoes he will step into in the morning.

Hills under the purple blur of autumn
are something he has never seen before.
White horse running for joy
hooves ploughing the ice-curded earth—
it asks no questions.

The sky stung by crows into sudden clamour
beyond the far fringe of branches,
black feathers sloughed from the ascending moon.

And the way small pools in the mud,
so many dark eyes,
wink up at him as he walks past,
crossing over from then to now as though
it were the easiest thing in the world.

NOTES AND DEDICATIONS

The epigraph to the book is by Izumi Shikibu, translated by Jane Hirshfield with Mariko Aratani, from *The Ink Dark Moon* (New York: Vintage Classics, 1990); used with the permission of Jane Hirshfield, all rights reserved.

Every line of "In Quarantine" alludes to the title of a different travel book.

"Emporium": Established in 1959, Gaynes Shoppers World was just off the I-89; it closed in the 1980s.

"Cathedral/Grove": Notre-Dame de Paris was built on the site of three earlier churches, themselves erected where a temple to Jupiter had been built by the Romans in 14 CE. Under that temple, archaeologists found an altar to both Roman and Gallic gods, which they dubbed "le Pilier des Nautes" ("the column of the sailors"). Now in the collection of the Musée de Cluny, it is attributed to the Parisii, a tribe conquered by the Romans in 52 BCE.

The poem is narrated by the presiding spirit of one of these tribesmen after fire ravaged the cathedral on April 15, 2019. The roof frame—known as "the forest" because it was built from 1,300 enormous wooden beams, each derived from a single oak—was completely destroyed. To have attained the requisite height by the time the cathedral was constructed in the 12th century, those trees would have to have been at least 300 to 400 years old. No matter how much money is raised by the devout and the sentimental, sufficient oak trees of this size no longer exist in France, or anywhere else on Earth, to replace what has been lost.

The title also alludes to "Cathedral Grove," otherwise known as MacMillan Provincial Park, one of the last remaining stands of old-growth forest on Vancouver Island. This sanctuary is situated in the traditional territory of the Tseshaht, Hupačasath, Nanoose, K'ómoks, Qualicum, Nanwakolas, and Te'mexw First Nations. Everywhere empires have invaded, their boots have crushed both nature and culture.

אייערלעך (pronounced eyerlekh): The literal meaning of the Yiddish word is "little eggs," but it refers specifically to the unhatched eggs found inside a slaughtered chicken.

Akedah (הקידה) means "binding" in Hebrew and refers to the story in Genesis 22 in which God asks that Abraham sacrifice his son, Isaac, to prove his obedience. Abraham binds Isaac and is about to slit his throat when an angel intervenes to stop him, and God provides an unfortunate ram to take the boy's place. I owe the insight into the role of Sarah to Rabbi Tina Grimberg.

Hineni (הנני) means "Here I am." It is a contraction of two Hebrew words: *hineh*, "here," and *ani*, "I."

"The Mermaid of Zennor" is depicted on a 500-year-old wooden bench inside the 1,400-year-old church of St. Senara in Cornwall, England. She was said to have attended services at the church for many years, never aging, enchanting everyone with her beautiful voice.

A "chimera" is a decorative architectural sculpture, generally of a grotesque creature, as opposed to a gargoyle, which is functional, acting as a drainpipe. All quotations are from *The Gar-*

goyles of Notre Dame: Medievalism and the Monsters of Modernity by Michael Camille (Chicago: University of Chicago Press, 2009).

The colour International Klein Blue was patented by the painter Yves Klein in 1960. The secret to its extraordinarily rich hue was the synthetic resin in which the pigment was suspended.

"After Pasternak" was written in response to the last line of Boris Pasternak's poem "Hamlet" from his novel *Dr. Zhivago*: "Life is not a walk across a field."

***

"A Mind of Winter" is for Julie Bruck.
"The Gloaming" is for Jane Hirshfield.
"La Floride" is for Toan Klein.
"Nurse Log" is for Carolyn Smart.
"Emporium" is for Laurence, Lisa, and David Glickman, who were there.
אייערלעך is for Simon Dardick.
"The Mermaid of Zennor" is for Helen Dunmore.
"Aquarium" is for Jesse and Rachel Klein.
"The Greenwood" is for Ruth Wyner.

ACKNOWLEDGEMENTS

Gratitude to the editors of the following journals and magazines in whose pages these poems first appeared, sometimes in different forms:

The Antigonish Review: "Green Tomatoes." *Arc*: "Potatoes," with accompanying drawing. *Canadian Literature*: "Hineni." *Event*: "Chimera," "The Apple." *Grain*: אייערלעך. *Juniper*: "Lettuce," with accompanying drawing. *The New Quarterly*: "Like Instruments," "The Greenwood," "What I Learned from Living Abroad," and the "Survival Kit" (about tools), *Prairie Fire*: "Unusually Warm for November," under the title "Mozart." *Religious Studies and Theology*: "Akedah." *Riddle Fence*: "After Completing the Cryptic Crossword, I Took the Dog for a Walk," "Daphne and Apollo." *Understory*: "Aquarium." *The Walrus*: "Frass."

"The Virus Enters the Body" was part of the Creation in Isolation project curated by Mark Raynes Roberts on Instagram.

"Nurse Log" appeared in *Worth More Standing*, an anthology of poems about trees, edited by Christine Lowther (Caitlin Press, 2022).

"After Pasternak" is from my first collection of poetry, *Complicity* (1983), now out of print.

Thanks are due to the Canada Council, the Ontario Arts Council, the Toronto Arts Council, *Arc* magazine, Guernica Press, *The New Quarterly*, and The Porcupine's Quill for financial support as well as encouragement and, for the latter, to the first and most generous reader of this manuscript, David O'Meara.

Much gratitude also to Mark Abley, Martha Baillie, Roo Borson, Julie Bruck, Julie Parker, Carolyn Smart, and Chantal Tie Ten Quee for reading and commenting on various poems in this collection, and to my family for putting up with my preoccupation and several burnt pots (sorry!) whilst I was writing them. And thanks, as always, to my wise and unflappable editor, Carmine Starnino, my equally genius cover designer, David Drummond, and to all the other lovely folks at Véhicule Press: Simon Dardick, Nancy Marrelli, Jennifer Varkonyi, and Patrick Goddard.

CARMINE STARNINO, EDITOR
MICHAEL HARRIS, FOUNDING EDITOR

Talya Rubin • Richard Sanger • Stephen Scobie
Peter Dale Scott • Deena Kara Shaffer
Carmine Starnino • Andrew Steinmetz • David Solway
Ricardo Sternberg • Shannon Stewart
Philip Stratford, trans. • Matthew Sweeney
Harry Thurston • Rhea Tregebov • Peter Van Toorn
Patrick Warner • Derek Webster • Anne Wilkinson
Donald Winkler, trans. • Shoshanna Wingate
Christopher Wiseman • Catriona Wright
Terence Young